IT'S ALL ABOUT...

SNAPPY
SHARKS

KINGFISHER
LONDON & NEW YORK

KINGFISHER
LONDON & NEW YORK

Copyright © Macmillan Publishers International Ltd 2016, 2020
First published in 2016 in the United States by Kingfisher
This edition published in 2020 by Kingfisher
120 Broadway, New York, NY 10271
Kingfisher is an imprint of Macmillan Children's Books, London

Distributed in the U.S. and Canada by Macmillan,
120 Broadyway, New York, NY 10271

Library of Congress Cataloging-in-Publication data has been applied for.

Series editor: Sarah Snashall
Series design: Anthony Hannant (LittleRedAnt) and Laura Hall
Illustrations: Laura Hall
Adapted from an original text by Anita Ganeri

ISBN 978-0-7534-7615-4

Kingfisher books are available for special promotions and premiums.
For details contact: Special Markets Department, Macmillan,
120 Broadway, New York, NY 10271

For more information, please visit www.kingfisherbooks.com

Printed in China
9 8 7 6 5 4 3 2 1
1TR/0620/WKT/UG/128MA

Picture credits
The Publisher would like to thank the following for permission to reproduce their materia
Top = t; Bottom = b; Center = c; Left = l; Right = r
Cover Shutterstock/Jim Agronick; background Shutterstock/PHOTOCREO Michal Bednarek
Back cover Shutterstock/Fiona Ayerst; Pages 3 Kingfisher Artbank; 4–5 Shutterstock/Rich
Carey; 5t Shutterstock/ShaunWilkinson; 6–7 Kingfisher Artbank; 6b Shutterstock/mj007;
8–9 Kingfisher Artbank; 8 Shutterstock/Fiona Ayerst; 10–11 Shutterstock/Matt9122;
11t Naturepl/Alex Hyde; 12 Shutterstock/Joost van Uffelen; 13t FLPA/R Dirschler;
13b Shutterstock/Kjersti Joergensen; 14 Photoshot/Tony Baskeyfield/NHPA; 15 Kingfisher
Artbank; 16–17 Shutterstock/Matt9122; 17 Alamy/Jeff Rotman; 18 Shutterstock/MP cz;
19 Alamy/Charles Hood; 20 Naturepl/Doug Perrine; 21 FLPA Flip Nicklin/Minden;
22–23 Shutterstock/Krzysztof Odziomek; 23 Shutterstock/Amanda Nicholls;
24 Shutterstock/Sergey Uryadnikov; 25 Shutterstock/Elsa Hoffmann; 26–27 Shutterstock/
Matt9122; 27tl Alamy/Peter Arnold Inc.; 27tr Shutterstock/Rich Carey; 28 Photolibrary;
29t FLPA Pete Oxford/Minden; 29 Shutterstock/Mark William Penny;
32 Shutterstock/Fiona Ayerst.

Front cover: A great white shark on the look-out for food.

CONTENTS

For your free audio download go to

http://panmacmillan.com/SnappySharks
or goo.gl/iBmzhH

Happy listening!

Scan me!

All shapes and sizes

There are more than 500 different species of shark, and they come in many shapes and sizes.

FACT...
The smallest shark is the dwarf lantern shark. It is only about the length of a pencil.

The sawshark has a flattened body and a long snout.

The mako shark has a powerful, streamlined body.

Some sharks are sleek hunters that speed through the water in search of their prey. Others, such as the whale shark, are giants that feed on tiny ocean creatures.

Prehistoric sharks

Sharks have been swimming in the oceans for more than 400 million years.

By the time the dinosaurs appeared, sharks had already been around for 200 million years!

Stethacanthus had a patch of small teeth on top of its head and on one fin.

Fossilized Megalodon tooth

Megalodon was a monster meat-eating shark that died out about 1.5 million years ago.

Stethacanthus

Megalodon

SPOTLIGHT: Megalodon

Record breaker:	largest-ever shark
Length:	up to 60 ft. (18m)
Teeth:	razor sharp
Ate:	whales and dolphins

Where do sharks live?

Sharks live in every part of the ocean, from the shallows to the deepest depths, and from rocky shores to coral reefs. Most are found in warm parts of the oceans. A few live in the cold oceans near the North and South poles.

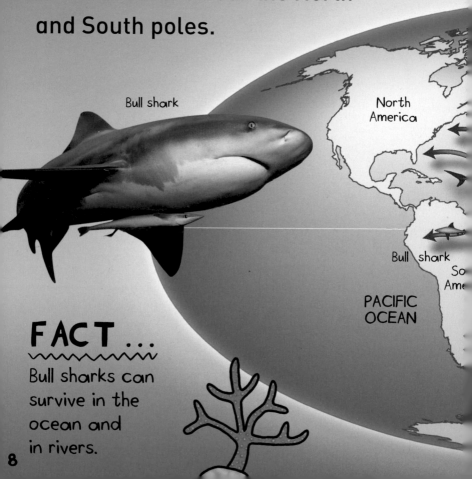

Bull shark

North America

Bull shark

So Ame

PACIFIC OCEAN

FACT...

Bull sharks can survive in the ocean and in rivers.

In winter in the Arctic, the ocean freezes over and the Greenland shark survives underneath the ice.

Some sharks travel long distances to find food and to breed. This is called migration.

Pole

nd

ARCTIC
OCEAN

and
k

Europe

ue
ark

Asia

Africa

Equator

INDIAN
OCEAN

LANTIC
CEAN

Great
white
shark

Australia

Antarctica

South Pole

9

Made for speed

Many sharks have a streamlined shape for fast swimming.

Jaws—for crushing

Teeth—very sharp and always growing

A shark's skeleton is not bony—it is made from rubbery cartilage. This makes the shark's body very flexible (bendy) as it swims.

Close-up view of shark skin

Gills—for breathing

Dorsal fin—for balance

Tail—for power

Pectoral fin—for steering

Skin—covered in teeth-like scales

FACT...

In the past, shark skin was used like sandpaper to make wood smooth.

Hide and seek

Most sharks are ocean colored. This helps them hide from their prey. Look at this blue shark. From above, it blends in with the dark ocean floor. From below, it is hidden against the bright surface of the water.

The wobbegong lies completely still on the seabed waiting for a tasty fish to swim by. Its shape and colors blend in with the sand, rocks, and seaweed.

This wobbegong is perfectly hidden.

FACT...

The spots on a leopard shark get lighter as the shark grows older.

On the move

When a shark swims, it moves its body from side to side. The shark uses its strong tail for power. It uses its fins to steer and stay upright.

SPOTLIGHT: Shortfin mako shark

Record breaker: fastest shark

Length: up to 13 ft. (4m)

Teeth: razor sharp

Eats: fish, squid, and other sharks

Different sharks have different-shaped tails. Some tails have evolved for fast swimming, others for cruising slowly after prey.

Tiger shark

Thresher shark

Swell shark

Sharks have a large liver filled with oil and fat to help them float.

Great white shark

FACT ...

Some sharks, such as sand tiger sharks, can store air in their stomach to help them float.

Shark senses

Sharks have very good eyesight and excellent hearing and smell. Sharks can hear sounds up to one mile (1.5 kilometers) away. Sharks can also pick up electrical signals and movement from nearby prey.

A hammerhead shark has eyes at each end of its hammer-shaped head.

Some sharks have an extra eyelid. This protects their eyes when they attack prey. Other sharks roll their eyes right back under their top eyelids.

This half-closed eye belongs to a Caribbean reef shark.

FACT...

A shark can smell blood from up to 450 yards (411 meters) away. They can detect one drop of blood in a million drops of water—that's enough water to fill your bathtub!

Scary hunters

Many sharks are fierce
predators that hunt fish, squid,
seals, dolphins, and turtles.
These sharks have a large
mouth lined with sharp teeth.
They swallow small animals
whole, or take huge bites out
of bigger prey.

Many sharks have
sharp teeth and
powerful jaws.

Not all sharks eat in this way. Some have a huge mouth but tiny teeth. They swim along with their mouth wide open, gulping in water and filtering out tiny fish and shrimps.

he 33-feet-long (10-meter-long) asking shark swims with its huge aws stretched wide open.

Baby sharks

Some sharks, such as blue sharks and lemon sharks, give birth to live babies, called pups.

Other sharks lay eggs in the water. The eggs have a tough case to protect them. Inside, the yolk provides food for the growing pup.

This lemon shark has just been born.

FACT...

Sometimes, empty egg cases wash up on the beach. They are known as "mermaids' purses."

Inside each of these egg cases is the embryo of a swell shark.

Monster shark!

Everything about the whale shark is ENORMOUS! It is not only the biggest shark, but it is also the biggest fish in the ocean. This giant can grow up to 50 feet (15 meters) long and weighs as much as three elephants.

SPOTLIGHT: Whale shark

Record breaker: largest living shark

Length: up to 50 ft. (15m)

Teeth: hundreds of tiny teeth

Eats: plankton, krill, and small fish

This human diver is tiny beside the whale shark.

As a filter feeder, the whale shark swims along slowly with its mouth wide open to catch shrimps and other tiny ocean animals.

FACT...

The whale shark's mouth is lined with more than 300 rows of tiny teeth.

Great white shark

The great white shark is the largest meat-eating shark in the ocean. It is a fierce and dangerous hunter.

FACT...

The great white shark sometimes lifts its head out of the water to see what is around it. This is called "spy-hopping."

A great white shark leaps out of the water to catch its prey.

The great white shark has jagged, razor-sharp teeth.

SPOTLIGHT: Great white shark

Record breaker: largest meat-eating shark
Length: up to 20 ft. (6m)
Teeth: about 300 razor-sharp teeth
Eats: fish, seals, sea lions, dolphins

Shark attacks

Some people think that all sharks are dangerous creatures that eat people. In fact, the chances of being attacked by a shark are very small. There are only about 80 shark attacks in the whole world each year, and fewer than 10 people are killed.

SPOTLIGHT: Tiger shark

Record breaker:	second most deadly to humans
Length:	about 16 ft. (5m)
Teeth:	sharp serrated teeth
Eats:	almost anything

A surfer

A turtle

From below, a person on a surfboard looks just like a turtle to a hungry tiger shark.

The tiger shark will swallow almost anything it finds, including garbage.

Sharks in danger

Every year, millions of sharks die because of humans. Some sharks are hunted, some are caught in fishing nets, and some are killed by pollution. Scientists are helping save sharks and their habitats.

FACT ...

Some sharks are killed for their fins, which are made into soup.

SAVE OUR SHARKS!

Scientists put tags on sharks to study how they behave.

82723

You can see some sharks in aquariums.

GLOSSARY

breed To have babies.

cartilage A tough, rubbery material that makes up a shark's skeleton.

cruising Traveling at a steady speed.

filter feeder A shark that swallows water and filters food out of the water through its gills.

fin Part of a fish's body that sticks up from its back, sides, or tail.

flexible Able to bend easily without breaking.

fossilized Describes the remains of a plant or animal that died millions of years ago and has been turned to stone.

gills Parts of the body used by some creatures to breathe underwater.

migration A long journey made by many animals to find places to feed and breed.

pollution Poisonous or harmful things in an environment.

predator An animal that hunts and kills other animals for food.

prehistoric From a long time ago, before history was written down.

prey An animal that is hunted and killed by other animals for food.

species A group of plants or animals that share similar features.

streamlined Having a shape that can move easily through water or air.

tag A marker or label that is attached to something.

yolk The part of an egg that provides food for the growing baby inside.

INDEX